P9-BYY-916

# SLAVERY AT MOUNT VERNON

By Janey Levy

Gareth Stevens
PUBLISHING

Please visit our website, www.garethstevens.com. For a free color catalog of all our high-quality books, call toll free 1-800-542-2595 or fax 1-877-542-2596.

**Library of Congress Cataloging-in-Publication Data**

Names: Levy, Janey., author.
Title: Slavery at Mount Vernon / Janey Levy.
Description: New York : Gareth Stevens Publishing, 2017. | Series: Hidden history | Includes index.
Identifiers: LCCN 2016028826| ISBN 9781482458022 (pbk. book) | ISBN 9781482458039 (6 pack) | ISBN 9781482458046 (library bound book)
Subjects: LCSH: Slaves–Virginia–Mount Vernon (Estate)–Juvenile literature. | Mount Vernon (Va. : Estate)–History–Juvenile literature. | Washington, George, 1732-1799–Relations with slaves–Juvenile literature.
Classification: LCC E312.5 .L475 2017 | DDC 306.3/6209755291–dc23
LC record available at https://lccn.loc.gov/2016028826

First Edition

Published in 2017 by
**Gareth Stevens Publishing**
111 East 14th Street, Suite 349
New York, NY 10003

Copyright © 2017 Gareth Stevens Publishing

Designer: Katelyn E. Reynolds
Editor: Therese Shea

Photo credits: Cover, pp. 1, 11 (inset) MPI/Getty Images; cover, pp. 1–32 (tear element) Shahril KHMD/Shutterstock.com; cover, pp. 1–32 (background texture) cornflower/ Shutterstock.com; cover, pp. 1–32 (background colored texture) K.NarlochLiberra/ Shutterstock.com; cover, pp. 1–32 (photo texture) DarkBird/Shutterstock.com; cover, pp. 1–32 (notebook paper) Tolga TEZCAN/Shutterstock.com; p. 5 (inset) baldeaglebluff/ Wikipedia.org; pp. 5 (main), 7, 9, 27 courtesy of the Library of Congress; p. 11 (main) Hulton Archive/Getty Images; pp. 12, 19 (inset) Edward Savage/Getty Images; p. 15 Independent Picture Service/UIG via Getty Images; p. 17 John Greim/LightRocket via Getty Images; p. 19 (main) Charles Phelps Cushing/ClassicStock/Getty Images; p. 21 Bettmann/Getty Images; p. 23 Joe Raedle/Getty Images; p. 25 Chicago History Museum/Getty Images; p. 29 Dennis K. Johnson/Lonely Planet Images/Getty Images.

Printed in the United States of America

CPSIA compliance information: Batch #CW17GS: For further information contact Gareth Stevens, New York, New York at 1-800-542-2595.

# CONTENTS

Words in the glossary appear in **bold** type the first time they are used in the text.

# EXCAVATIONS
## AT THE HOUSE FOR FAMILIES

In 1989 and 1990, archaeologists excavated the site where Mount Vernon's House for Families once stood. It was the main slave **quarters** at the Mansion House Farm, George Washington's residence. The discoveries shed new light on the lives of the slaves who dwelled there.

The **artifacts** uncovered—including **ceramics**, glass, tobacco pipes, and table **utensils**—suggested the slaves received material benefits from living so near Washington's family. Yet the fact remains that they were slaves.

Mount Vernon holds a special place in US history and in the hearts of many Americans. But its history of slavery has remained largely hidden until recently. That's because it's difficult to accept the **contradiction** of a Founding Father who fought for liberty, but engaged in the practice of slavery.

### REVEALED

Washington's Mount Vernon estate was divided into five separate farms: Mansion House Farm, Dogue Run Farm, River Farm, Muddy Hole Farm, and Union Farm. The Mansion House Farm—the largest farm—was centered around the mansion, Washington's stately home shown in images of Mount Vernon.

# MORE FROM THE HOUSE FOR FAMILIES EXCAVATION

Archaeologists believe a number of the artifacts uncovered were probably handed down to the slaves from the Washingtons. Slaves may have made others themselves. In addition to the artifacts, archaeologists uncovered more than 24,000 bones from 53 kinds of animals. The food remains indicate slaves were adding to the **rations** they received. Their regular rations were herring, cornmeal, beef, and pork. The remains show slaves hunted wild game, fished, gardened, gathered nuts and berries, and raised chickens.

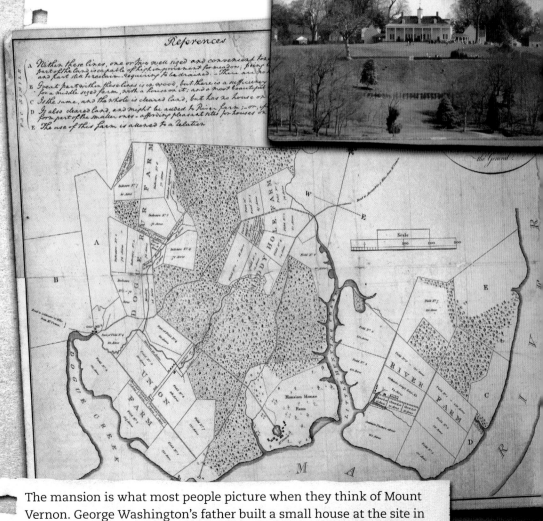

The mansion is what most people picture when they think of Mount Vernon. George Washington's father built a small house at the site in 1735. George's brother Lawrence added to the house after it became his in 1743, and George enlarged it still more after Lawrence's death.

# GEORGE WASHINGTON AND SLAVERY

People have long known Washington had slaves; numerous **documents** provide evidence. But the subject hasn't received much public attention until recently. Now, however, people recognize it's important to discuss slavery at Mount Vernon and Washington's attitude toward it.

Washington grew up in a society that treated slavery as a normal part of life. He inherited 10 slaves at the age of 11 when his father died. As a young adult, he purchased at least eight slaves. He bought seven more slaves in 1755, including a child.

Washington's marriage to the widow Martha Dandridge Custis in 1759 brought 84 more slaves to Mount Vernon. The slave population at Mount Vernon also increased through the purchase of more slaves and through children born to slaves.

## REVEALED

Someone who borrowed money from Washington failed to pay back the loan. So Washington took that person's slaves—including children—and sold them to the highest bidder.

# A VISITOR'S VIEW

In 1798, a Polish visitor spent 12 days at Mount Vernon and wrote this about Washington and his slaves: "General Washington treats his slaves far more humanely [compassionately] than do his fellow citizens of Virginia." But he also wrote, "We entered one of the huts of the Blacks, for one cannot call them by the name of houses. They are more miserable than the most miserable of the cottages of our peasants."

Washington is shown here speaking with an overseer, a man in charge of the slaves on one of the farms at Mount Vernon. Overseers might be free white men or selected slaves.

Washington commonly separated the husbands and wives in his slave population. Skilled males were housed close to the mansion, while their wives and children were on the outer farms. About 65 percent of the field slaves were women.

Washington approved harsh punishments, which he called corrections, for even minor offenses. However, he also watched the health of his slaves and even took ill slaves to the mansion so they could be cared for.

The American Revolution changed Washington's views on slavery. He witnessed the courage of black soldiers fighting in the Continental army. He was also exposed to the antislavery views of the Marquis de Lafayette. While he never publicly supported the abolition of slavery, he hoped Congress would end it. And in his will, he ordered all his slaves to be freed after his wife's death.

## WASHINGTON'S WILL

In his will, Washington wrote: "Upon the decease [death] of my wife, it is my Will & desire that all the Slaves which I hold in my own right, shall receive their freedom." However, only 123 of the 317 slaves then at Mount Vernon belonged to him. Most of the rest were Martha's and legally belonged to her first husband's estate. They would return to the Custis family after Martha's death. Neither George nor Martha had the right to free them.

Washington once approved the whipping of a household worker for being impertinent, or disrespectful: "If She, or any other of the Servants will not do their duty by fair means, or are impertinent, correction (as the only alternative) must be administered."

The Marquis de Lafayette (right) was a wealthy young French nobleman who came to America to support the colonies in the American Revolution. He and Washington became close friends. Lafayette strongly supported the right of people to rule themselves and firmly opposed slavery.

# SLAVE LABOR

What was it like to work as a slave at Mount Vernon? Usually, slaves worked from sunrise to sunset, with about 2 hours off for meals. That meant slaves worked about 8 hours a day during the winter, when there are fewer hours of daylight. During the summer, when days are longer, slaves might work as much as 14 hours a day.

Slaves labored 6 days a week, with Sundays off. They also received a few holidays a year. However, when a job such as harvesting had to be completed within a limited time, slaves had to work through their days off. When the job was finished, they might receive money or another day off to make up for time off they missed.

## REVEALED

Many of the holidays the slaves received were Christian holidays such as Christmas and Easter. However, not all slaves were Christians. Some continued to practice religious traditions brought from Africa, such as Islam.

# THE VERY YOUNG AND VERY OLD

According to the slave list put together in 1799, about 42 percent, or nearly half, of Mount Vernon's slaves were too young or too old to work. There were also slaves whose physical abilities didn't allow them to do very hard, demanding labor. They were often given jobs such as making clothing or shoes or picking wild onion seeds out of the store of oat seeds.

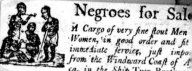

Negroes for Sale

A Cargo of very fine stout Men and Women, in good order and fit for immediate service, just imported from the Windward Coast of Africa, in the Ship Two Brothers.—Conditions are one half Cash or Produce, the other half payable the first of January next, giving Bond and Security if required.

The Sale to be opened at 10 o'Clock each Day, at Mr. Bourdeaux's Yard, at No. 48, on the Bay.

May 19, 1784.          JOHN MITCHELL.

Thirty Seasoned Negroes

To be Sold for Credit, at Private Sale.

AMONGST which is a Carpenter, none of whom are known to be dishonest.

Also, to be sold for Cash, a regular bred young Negroe Man-Cook, born in this Country, who served several Years under an exceeding good French Cook abroad, and his Wife a middle aged Washer-Woman, (both very honest) and their two Children.—Likewise, a young Man a Carpenter.

For Terms apply to the Printer.

This image shows Washington visiting his slaves while they work in the fields. As the advertisements above make clear, most people at this time viewed slaves as property to be bought and sold. Washington shared this view for most of his life.

For slaves, work at the mansion was preferred to the much harsher work in the fields. More than once, Washington threatened to punish house slaves by sending them to the fields when he felt they weren't doing their work.

This painting shows George and Martha at Mount Vernon with two of Martha's grandchildren.

Of the 58 percent of Mount Vernon's slaves who were able to work, slightly more than 25 percent were skilled laborers. They worked as house servants, blacksmiths, barrel makers, cooks, dairymaids, **distillers**, gardeners, millers, **seamstresses**, shoemakers, spinners, knitters, ditch diggers, wagon drivers, or carriage drivers. They were housed close to the mansion, and almost 75 percent of them were men.

Nearly 75 percent of the working slaves toiled in the fields, and most were women. The work they did was hard, demanding physical labor. They hoed, plowed, and harvested. They collected and spread manure. They pulled tree stumps out of the ground. They built fences around Mount Vernon. And remember—in summer, they might have done this for 14 hours a day.

## WASHINGTON'S HOUSEHOLD STAFF

Like other wealthy Virginians, Washington preferred to use lighter-skinned mixed-race slaves as his household staff. These individuals had mixed ancestry, which means a parent, or perhaps a grandparent, had been a white person. One visitor to Mount Vernon wrote of meeting a boy with such fair hair and skin color "that if I had not been told, I should never have suspected his [African] ancestry."

# SLAVE QUARTERS

Remember the House for Families mentioned in the first chapter? It was the quarters for house slaves and skilled workers on the Mansion House Farm. It offered perhaps the nicest slave quarters at Mount Vernon in terms of quality of construction. It was a two-story wooden building with a brick foundation, a **chimney** at each end, and glass windows. However, slaves living there had little privacy from each other and from their nearby "owner."

The House for Families was torn down in the 1790s. Beginning around 1793, most of the Mansion House Farm slaves lived in brick wings flanking the greenhouse. The wings contained a total of four large rooms, each with a fireplace, built-in beds, and glass windows. Here, too, slaves had little privacy.

## REVEALED

The greenhouse and the attached slave quarters were destroyed by fire twice, in 1835 and again in 1863.

# MORE ABOUT
# THE GREENHOUSE SLAVE QUARTERS

Each room had a single door to the outside and provided about 600 square feet (55 sq m) of living space. As many as 60 slaves may have lived in the quarters, so it's likely 15 lived in each room. It's believed the quarters were designed to house adults who didn't have families with them. Some slaves also lived in rooms above the kitchen building, and families had individual cabins across from the greenhouse.

This image gives you an idea of what some of the slave quarters at Mount Vernon were like.

The slaves on Mount Vernon's other farms had more privacy. For one thing, they lived much farther from Washington and his watchful eye. For another, they lived in either their own cabin or a cabin meant to house two families in separate spaces. However, the quality of construction was much poorer than at the House for Families or the Greenhouse Slave Quarters.

One visitor described these cabins as "log-houses." They were smeared with mud in an unsuccessful effort to keep out wind and rain. A cabin for one family had a single room and often a wooden chimney made of sticks plastered with mud on an exterior wall. A cabin for two families had two rooms, each with its own entrance, separated by a chimney in the middle.

## A VISITOR'S ACCOUNT

A man who visited Washington at Mount Vernon left an account of the interior of a slave cabin. Keep in mind that a single small room served as living room, kitchen, and bedroom: "The husband and wife sleep on a mean pallet, the children on the ground; a very bad fireplace, some utensils for cooking, but in the middle of this poverty some cups and a teapot."

This reconstructed, or rebuilt, slave cabin provides an idea of the kind of living quarters most of Mount Vernon's slaves occupied.

# SLAVE CLOTHING

Washington provided clothing for his slaves, but he supplied the least amount possible, and it was plain and often coarse. Most slaves received clothing annually, plus an additional item or two as necessary for the changing seasons. Since slaves received few items of clothing, they often wore the same clothes day after day. The poorest clothing went to children and adults too old to work. In fact, an overseer reported one December that children on one farm had no clothes.

Some clothing was made from cloth produced at Mount Vernon or imported cloth, while some was ordered ready-made in large quantities. Fabrics included wool and unbleached coarse linen called osnaburg. Washington complained when a seamstress made long pants for the men instead of short breeches because they used too much cloth.

## REVEALED

Slaves also received blankets occasionally. But Washington ordered them to use their blankets to gather leaves for livestock beds, which he said was necessary "for the comfort of the Creatures . . . Make the Cattle lay warm and comfortable. The hogs also in pens must be well bedded in leaves."

# HOUSE SLAVES' CLOTHING

House slaves received more clothing of better quality than field slaves. Male slaves wore suits known as liveries that were modeled after the three-piece suits worn by gentlemen of the time. Liveries were commonly made of fine wool in the colors of the owner's **coat of arms**. Elaborately woven lace decorated the edges. Female slaves wore dresses of fine cloth, with an apron of delicate linen called lawn.

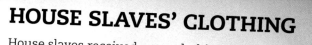

William Lee, Washington's personal slave

This image gives an idea of how Washington's field slaves would have been dressed in summer. The men wear just a simple shirt and pants. Washington's slaves, however, would likely have worn shorter breeches.

# THE PRIVATE LIVES OF SLAVES

What did Mount Vernon's slaves do when they weren't working? The most important daily activities were housekeeping chores. The slaves kept small gardens and raised chickens to add to the rations Washington provided them. They needed to tend the chickens and gardens, cook and preserve what they got from their gardens, and do what was necessary to care for their clothing, such as cleaning and mending.

The chickens, the eggs they laid, and the produce from the garden could provide the slaves with income as well. Washington himself purchased food from his slaves, as well as items such as brooms the slaves had made. The slaves also sold the food and goods they made at the Sunday market in Alexandria.

## REVEALED

A Mount Vernon visitor described the scene around a slave's cabin: "A very small garden planted with vegetables was close by, with five or six hens, each one leading 10 to 15 chickens. It is the only comfort that is permitted them; for they may not keep either ducks, geese, or pigs."

# OTHER WAYS TO EARN MONEY

Some slaves earned money through fishing and hunting. Washington enjoyed fish and would pay handsomely for fine ones. Mount Vernon slaves Tom Davis and Sambo Anderson were well-known hunters and sold Washington 132 birds in the fall of 1792. When Anderson received his freedom after Washington's death, he supported himself by hunting wild game and selling it to hotels. Other slaves sold their teeth to dentists for use in **dentures** and in tooth transplant operations!

This painting shows several slaves at a cabin. One woman is washing in a wooden tub, and one sits mending. Chickens surround the small cabin.

What did Mount Vernon slaves do with the money they earned? Some, such as the Washingtons' chef Hercules, spent it on better clothing. Hercules was renowned for his cooking skill. He accompanied them to Philadelphia, the nation's capital at the time, while Washington served as president. There, he earned up to $200 a year selling leftovers from the kitchen. This income allowed him to purchase fine white linen, a black silk waistcoat, a blue cloth coat with a velvet collar, and a gold-headed cane—clothing far superior to that of even the most favored house slave.

Other slaves preferred to buy food. They purchased items from Washington such as fine flour and pork. They also purchased imported foods such as tea, coffee, molasses, and sugar from shops in Alexandria.

## HOME SWEET HOME

Slaves also used their money to purchase furniture and other items for their dwellings. Surviving legal documents provide a lengthy list of items one woman acquired for her home. That list includes a desk, three tables, eight chairs, two mirrors, 13 pictures, 18 plates, six teacups, a sugar dish, a cream pot, and two beds. That's remarkable compared to the furnishings of the average slave dwelling.

The Washingtons called Hercules "Uncle Harkless." Martha's grandson described him as "a celebrated artiste . . . as highly accomplished a proficient [expert] in the culinary [cooking] art as could be found in the United States."

This is the dining room at Mount Vernon, where the Washingtons would have eaten meals prepared for them by Hercules.

In addition to earning money and making purchases, the slaves tried to enjoy their free time. A favorite activity was visiting each other at night, after they had finished work for the day. The slaves on the outer farms went from cabin to cabin to see each other. Washington complained they were too tired after what he called "night walking" to do the work he expected them to do.

They also went swimming and played games and sports. A visitor to Mount Vernon observed 30 slaves playing a team sport called "prisoner's base." The visitor noted the slaves played the athletic game with great enthusiasm, engaging in "jumps and gambols [leaps] as if they had rested all week."

Slave life was cruel, but the slaves were determined to create good times.

## VISITING DISTANT FAMILY

Some husbands and wives were separated because they worked on different farms at Mount Vernon. Others were married to people who lived on different plantations. These couples could only visit each other on days off—Sundays and holidays. And sometimes they couldn't even do that. A slave owner might decide to forbid slaves from other plantations from coming to his plantation.

The slaves' visits with each other included music and storytelling. Slaves who had been born in Africa told stories about life in that distant land.

Here, slaves have gathered outside their cabins to enjoy each other's company, listen to music, and dance.

# HOW SLAVES RESISTED

Mount Vernon slaves resisted slavery in various ways. They faked illness, worked slowly, did poor work, and misplaced or damaged tools and equipment. Any slave, regardless of age or state of health, could resist by these means, and it was hard to prove they did these things on purpose.

Theft was another means of resistance. It was more dangerous because slaves were more likely to be caught and punished. Slaves were accused of stealing tools, fabrics, milk, butter, fruits, meats, corn, potatoes, and more. Washington himself detected a scheme to steal wool by claiming it was too dirty to spin: "I perceive [observe] by the Spinning Report of last week, that each of the spinners have deducted [removed] half a pound for dirty wool."

Of course, the greatest expression of resistance was escape.

## REVEALED

So much seed disappeared from Mount Vernon that Washington ordered it to be mixed with sand, making it harder to steal.

## ESCAPE!

Escape was the most dramatic and powerful form of resistance. Seventeen slaves escaped Mount Vernon during the American Revolution when a British warship was anchored nearby. Supplies were offered to the ship in exchange for the slaves, but the captain refused to return them. Somewhat to the puzzlement of the Washingtons, the desire for freedom was so strong that house slaves who enjoyed privileged positions—Hercules, the chef, and Martha's personal maid, Oney (Ona) Judge—both escaped.

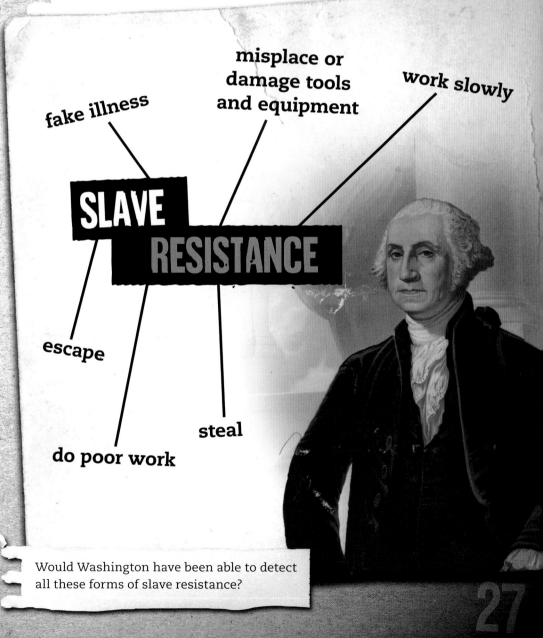

fake illness

misplace or damage tools and equipment

work slowly

# SLAVE RESISTANCE

escape

do poor work

steal

Would Washington have been able to detect all these forms of slave resistance?

# DIGGING UP
## MOUNT VERNON'S PAST

Archaeologists continue to work on learning more about Mount Vernon's history of slavery. In 2014, they began a multiyear project to excavate the Slave Burial Ground. It's especially important because so little is known about the burial ground. In fact, it was never mentioned during Washington's lifetime.

The earliest account comes from the journal of a woman who visited Mount Vernon in 1833, when the Washington family still owned it. She wrote that near Washington's tomb "you see the burying place of his slaves."

It's not even known how many graves are in the burial ground. The 1833 account mentions 150 graves. An account from 1838 says 100 graves. It's hoped the project can locate all the graves and thus honor the slaves who lived and died at Washington's home.

### REVEALED

Entrance to Mount Vernon is free for anyone wishing to visit the Slave Burial Ground on Thursdays and Fridays. If you're at least 16, you can also volunteer to help on the excavation.

# NAMING NAMES

It's possible graves in the Slave Burial Ground once had markers with names, but any such markers are long gone. However, it's believed certain well-known slaves were buried there, including William Lee, Washington's personal servant, and Frank Lee, William's brother and Mount Vernon's butler. It's also believed West Ford, a longtime servant of the Washington family who died at Mount Vernon in 1863, was the last person buried there.

This marker honoring the slaves buried in Mount Vernon's Slave Burial Ground was erected in 1983.

# GLOSSARY

**artifact:** something made by humans in the past

**ceramics:** useful objects made from clay and then fired at high temperatures

**chimney:** a vertical structure that is part of a building and is designed to carry off the smoke from a fireplace

**coat of arms:** a design of symbols standing for a family, city, or country

**contradiction:** conflict, disagreement

**denture:** a set of false teeth

**distiller:** a person who produces alcoholic drinks through a process that involves heating liquids to concentrate them

**document:** a formal piece of writing

**quarters:** the housing occupied by a group

**rations:** food, provisions

**seamstress:** a woman who sews by hand to make and repair clothes, curtains, and household linens

**utensil:** an article that is useful or necessary in a household, such as a spoon or a knife

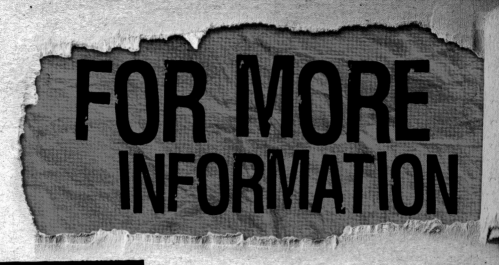

# FOR MORE INFORMATION

## BOOKS

Delano, Marfé Ferguson. *Master George's People: George Washington, His Slaves, and His Revolutionary Transformation.* Washington, DC: National Geographic, 2013.

Santella, Andrew. *Mount Vernon.* Minneapolis, MN: Compass Point Books, 2005.

Turner, Diane D. *My Name Is Oney Judge.* Chicago, IL: Third World Press, 2010.

## WEBSITES

**George Washington's Mount Vernon for Students**
*www.mountvernon.org/education/for-students/*
Explore Mount Vernon, the colonial era, George Washington's life, primary sources, and more on this amazing site!

**Mount Vernon, Virginia**
*www.nps.gov/nr/travel/presidents/mount_vernon.html*
Read about the history of Mount Vernon and the Washington family on this website.

# INDEX